PPC Profit

Learn The Techniques Of
Pay-Per-Click And Get
The Maximum Traffic To Your Website

Vixen Dorf

DISCLAIMER

This information is provided and sold with the knowledge that the publisher and author do not offer any legal or other professional advice. In the case of a need for any such expertise consult with the appropriate professional. This book does not contain all information available on the subject. This book has not been created to be specific to any individual's or organizations' situation or needs. Every effort has been made to make this book as accurate as possible. However, there may be typographical and or content errors. Therefore, this book should serve only as a general guide and not as the ultimate source of subject information. This book contains information that might be dated and is intended only to educate and entertain. The author and publisher shall have no liability or responsibility to any person or entity regarding any loss or damage incurred, or alleged to have incurred, directly or indirectly, by the information contained in this book.

Thank you for downloading this book. Please review on Amazon for us so that I can make future versions even better. A portion of the proceeds from this book goes to American Cancer Society®. Thank you for you support. God bless.

Just for Downloading this book and showing your support, I wanna give you 2 of our other books, absolutely **FREE**. Just go to the link and subscribe and get **2 Free Books** for your support. Don't forget to give us **5 star Rating** so we can make better versions to help more people. Thank you guys for your support.

Click Here to Download-Free Website Traffic & How To Invest in The Stock Market

Table of Contents

Google AdWords – An Overview

Google AdWords is a pay-per-click solution offered by Google. Pay per click type of advertising can help transform your web site from no traffic to web site with high traffic. This can bring in huge profits. Google AdWords offers easy solutions and techniques to get the maximum traffic to your web site very quickly.

Pay per click advertising requires you to form a small advertisement covering barely two to three lines. This carries a headline citing your keyword. Clicking on this headline provides link to your web site. Ideally, Google.com offers organic results and paid links for every search on the web site. Paid links normally appear on the right hand side while organic results are on the left.

Every time anybody clicks on your paid advertisements at Google site, you pay a fee to Google. Fees can be anything from .10 cents to many dollars depending on the demand and popularity of your keyword. You should target quality clicks at your web site to increase sales and pay your advertisement costs too.

Google offers a certain AdRank to monitor the Google AdWords at the web site. The three main governing factors are keywords or phrases, bid price, and the quality score. Aim to project your advertisement on the first few pages, as people normally do not scout beyond these while on their search.

Such projection requires a targeted keyword. The keyword should bear a direct link to your product. Put your keyword within quotes if you want the searched keywords to appear in that order. There are only ten available slots for sponsored links at the first page of Google web site. Therefore, make use of the Google AdWords Keyword Finder to find the best and most appropriate keyword for your product.

Locate the going rate for your chosen keyword and the projected bid amount too. Choose your bid position according to the cost savings accruing to you. Relevance of the particular keyword and its performance in the past determine the quality score of the keyword. Overall, all these factors determine your advertisement costs and how much you gain through such advertisements in the form of increased sales.

Success of Google AdWords

Google AdWords has been very successful. Click through ads was not so popular previously. However, with the advent of Google AdWords click through rates have increased by around two percent. Resultant conversion rates have also increased by around 15% in the United Kingdom market.

Google AdWords helps project your advertisements with targeted keywords. Although this has lowered the number of searches, yet it has been able to generate high click through rates.

No doubt, Google ranks as the most popular and largest search engine on the Internet. It has around eight billion web pages and functions in more than a hundred different languages. You can use the many different tools available on Google to expedite your search. Google projects a clean interface with many different image databases.

Google is into partnerships with many different web sites. Therefore, your advertisements have a chance to appear on many different sites. You can choose the necessary sites for display of your advertisements. Google helps in setting up your account, offers many interesting tutorials, and answers your queries within seconds.

Google offers another great incentive. If you have a high click through rate in your ads, you pay less for the higher ranks. You can test the different texts of your advertisements and receive more clicks at low costs. If your advertisements do not perform well, even bidding at high levels cannot prove beneficial.

What are Google AdWords?

Google offers an advertisement service on its web site and partner sites too. This text-based advertising service is Google AdWords. This requires you to form your own advertisements through targeted keywords. These keywords should relate directly to your product. You incur advertisement costs only if people click at your advertisement. You do not have to pay anything to Google for displaying your advertisement.

Google displays Google AdWords alongside the free search results on its web site for any particular keyword. Therefore, your AdWords could be for the entire range of your products or for any specific product too.

Most Internet marketers consider Google AdWords to be a form of direct marketing. This is because you are able to deliver your message across to individual potential customers. Besides, this form of advertisement is very cost-effective.

You can advertise for as little as $1.50 for a month. You incur an initial cost of $5 as signing up charges at AdWords. Thereafter, you can keep your budget to even as low as five cents each day.

Google does not offer any set price for advertising through AdWords. You have to bid on your keywords. The highest bidder gets the topmost position on the sponsored links section of Google web site. However, Google places maximum importance on the effective advertisements. Therefore, highest bidder may not always find the topmost place.

How Google AdWords Works

Google AdWords is an enhancement of its Pay per Click advertising system. Google AdWords helps you reach targeted audience to market your products. If you want to advertise on Google, you have to first draft the particular advertisement according to Google specifications.

The headline should ideally be the targeted keyword or phrase but do not use any superlatives. You can follow it up with a two-line brief description, your URL, and then that of your page.

You pay an activation fee of $5. The minimum cost for a click on the keyword starts from five cents. This also depends on the popularity of the keyword and your ranking on Google. Google sets different costs for different ad groups.

If the cost per click you specify for your ad is higher than the cost of the group, you pay only the actual cost applicable. You do not have to pay the higher cost. Google offers simple tools like Traffic Estimator to help you determine the cost of any particular keyword. The cost of your advertisement also depends on the click through rate. If your advertisement is more effective than another advertisement, Google gives a higher ranking to your advertisement with increase in your targeted cost. However, you pay only what you originally chose as the cost of your advertisement. Google gives you a daily report of the number of times your advertisement was on its web site.

Why Google AdWords?

Google AdWords helps you reach a wide section of people. Google is accessible by more than eighty percent of regular Internet users. You can get the best exposure for your ads at Google"s search page. There are around 2.73 million users on any particular day with around 81.9 million unique users in a month.

Additionally, advertising on Google helps you connect to several other search engines like Netscape, AOL, Earth Link, About.com, Lowestfare.com, FoxSports.com, Shopping. com, and many more. Google also processes a set of content specific AdWords for display on AdSense, an affiliate program of Google. You also benefit from Google e-mail service of Gmail. Your advertisements also appear on the messages on Gmail, which is an additional exposure for your products.

Your advertisement should be very impressive and compelling for people to click at it. This helps you optimize your listings and rank higher than other products. Google offers excellent tools for choosing the best keyword for your product like WordTracker. This tool helps analyze your chosen keyword to include all relevant information of your product. Google AdWords supports many different programming languages and environment like Perl, Java, PHP, .NET, and others. Signing up at Google does not include any long and laborious processes. Creating and activating a My Client Center account will enable you to go ahead with writing of your advertisements soon.

What is Pay Per Click?

Pay per click advertising is a type of advertising on the different search engines. This helps you search and locate the correct keywords for your product. You can also choose the charges you would pay for every click on your advertisement. Obviously, the higher you are able to pay for each click, the higher your site appears on the search results of keywords. Pay per click is the same as cost per click.

There are many different search engines on the Internet allowing such pay per click advertising. The largest in the pay per click industry are Google and Yahoo! Although Google is not a pay per click search engine, it does allow for such pay per click advertising in the boxes adjacent to the search results for any keyword. Additionally, it provides such pay per click advertisements to its affiliate sites and other content sites too. While opting for pay per click advertising, you have to start with little investment. This will help you gauge performance of your search engine. You can analyze the targeted traffic at your web site and consider the conversion rates of this traffic into paying customers.

Before choosing any particular search engine for pay per click advertising, you have to collect details of the search engine. Essentially, check if the search engine has a perfect mechanism to check fraudulent clicks.

Differences between Google AdWords and Yahoo Overture

Yahoo Overture and Google AdWords offer pay per click advertising. Yahoo operates through Yahoo Search Marketing. However, there exists major differences in their working and resultant performances.

Bidding: Yahoo gives all details of your advertisement costs, your rankings, and payments. Yahoo"s maximum bid is at $999.99 and lowest at $0.10. Google does not disclose details of your bid or that of the competitors. You do not know how much you have to pay per click. The maximum bid is $100 and minimum is $0.05.

However, Google places you at a higher position if your click rate is higher than your competitor is, even though your bid is lower.

Languages: Google helps you choose your country and language through a drop down box. The language is according to the visitor"s computer. Yahoo does not offer any such thing. You have to register for every country and language, which makes things difficult. You have to resubmit all information at every new site, which is too cumbersome.

Reports: Google mails you customized reports regularly. With Yahoo, you have to select the report you want.

Yahoo presents a low cost rate than Google but conversion rate is higher in Google. Ideally, the conversion rate of your clicks is more important for deciding your total sales and profits. Therefore, Google helps you get more targeted traffic at your web site.

Google AdWords vs. Traditional Advertising

The Internet has opened many new opportunities for advertising. The traditional method of advertising in radio, television, magazines, and newspapers is taking a back seat. Only few could afford such advertisements for their products and services. Otherwise, you had to scout for some other means of advertising your product and reaching a wider clientele.

Google AdWords offer content-based advertising. Such advertising delivers to targeted audience and proves very beneficial to you. Traditional advertising methods do not offer any targeted advertising.

Google AdWords offers you detailed analysis of how many visitors came to your site at any particular time, the number of hits at your advertisement, and how many of these hits convert into sales. It is almost impossible to calculate the number of viewers viewing your advertisements through newspapers, television, or other traditional forms of advertising.

Google AdWords is affordable by most, as you only have to pay $5 for activating your account. Thereafter, charges for your advertisements are on performance basis. You pay only if visitors click on your advertisements. Besides, bidding costs for your advertisements are as low as a nickel. However, a small advertisement on the yellow-page costs nothing less than many hundreds of dollars.

Google AdWords has a greater range as the Internet can reach many millions of people across the globe. People from any corner of the world can view your advertisement. Traditional advertising techniques restrict viewership, as books, magazines, television, and radio cater according to regional and other geographical boundaries.

You can also determine the maximum amount of money you want to spend on advertising each day. Google AdWords has a discounter feature to monitor the highest bids and therefore, you do not have to overspend for making your advertisements appear at the top of the listings. Higher conversion rates at Google AdWords further lowers your expenses on advertisements. Google AdWords offers extensive flexibility and you can make any number of changes in your advertisements at any time you feel like. Although Google AdWords does score over traditional advertising, still you can opt for traditional advertising methods in select areas.

Before You Start Your
Google AdWords Campaign

Before starting on your Google AdWords campaign, you have to gain sufficient knowledge about working of the campaign with in-depth information about pay per click, click through rates, and similar others. The Internet itself offers many opportunities to gain information through eBooks and relevant sites offering many different tips and strategies.

After educating yourself, you can open a Google AdWords account. You need to write a creative advertisement to grab the attention of people visiting your web site. Your web site should be attractive in features and content too. Appropriate landing pages for your products and services are essential. You can decide on having many different pages if you have more than one product or service. Then your landing page is one of the pages on your web site. Alternatively, your main web site or web page could be your landing page. Write out many different advertisements and try their effectiveness by testing the click through rate of each advertisement.

A focused and targeted keyword list can bring in more traffic at your web site. You also need to fix a budget according to your affordability levels. The amount you are willing to pay for every click should ideally depend on the type of traffic you receive at your site. If you receive focused traffic with high conversion rates, it can prove beneficial for you. Therefore, your advertisement decides the traffic, which in turn is the key factor in deciding your budget.

If you want to develop sales leads, your landing page should have proper channels for people to ask for further information. Such information should ideally reach a lead capture form containing essential details for processing of the lead. This also helps in developing a suitable customer relationship management.

However, your lead should also find it easy to approach you through telephone, e-mail, or any other form of contact too for any further clarifications or information. You can check on this aspect of easy accessibility before starting with your Google AdWords campaign.

What AdWords Ads Cost

Google AdWords charge a $5 activation fee to open and activate your Google account. The minimum amount is $.01 for a single click. Google AdWords bills you for clicks only after they accumulate to $50 to $150.

If there are no clicks on your advertisement, you do not have to pay anything. Google AdWords does not charge you for displaying your advertisement.

Google AdWords follows a bidding system for fixing the cost of your advertisement. The highest bidder with the best quality score occupies the topmost position in their advertisements. Google AdWords does not charge any monthly minimum charges. Google AdWords proves beneficial to small businesses specifically in reaching extensive markets.

Opening Your Google AdWords Account

The first step is to log into AdWords site of Google and select suitable country and language according to your preferences. Click on the save and continue button after posting details on every page.

Name your advertisement group and make your advertisement at Create Ads section. You can always edit your advertisements. Google immediately gives a preview of your advertisement.

Use the Keyword Suggestion Tool link to locate the most suitable and ideal keyword for your advertisement. Check its suitability for targeting huge traffic. Choose the minimum bid amount of $0.05 as your maximum initially. You can later change the bid amount depending on the traffic. You have to specify your daily budget on your advertisements now.

After clicking on the save and continue button, provide your contact details and password. Give your valid e-mail address to complete the final step of confirmation and billing. After clicking on the relevant button, you receive a thank you message from Google for registering at the site. You can then find a mail from Google at your e-mail with a link to their verification process.

After verification and checking of the validity of your e-mail, Google forwards a message for activation of your account. You have to give your payment details for running your advertisements. After you submit this information, Google activates your AdWords account. Almost immediately, you can locate traffic at your web site.

How is Your Google AdWords Ads Display Position Determined?

Google uses a unique way to determine position of your advertisement on its site. Google uses a two-tier system to decide positioning of your advertisement. It is normally according to the bidding amounts for these positions and the click through rate of your advertisement.

The cost per click of your advertisement is the amount you bid and are ready to pay. You can better your position by paying a higher cost per click in relation to what other listed advertisements are paying. However, once you achieve this position on the Google AdWords, you have to maintain it too.

Maintaining your position on the Google AdWords depends on your click through rate. If your advertisement records many clicks, your can carry on with your position. However, if the click rate falls below permitted levels of Google, you lose your position and ranking on the Google site.

Therefore, your ranking on the Google AdWords is the product of the maximum cost per click and click through rate. If any two advertisers have the same ranking, Google AdWords determines your position by calculating any number of decimal places as necessary. It is a wrong notion that the highest bidder will reign at the topmost position on Google AdWords. Google reviews your keywords to decide on your position.

How is a Google AdWords Campaign Structured?

Google AdWords campaign has three levels: campaign, AdWords, and advertisements. You can choose the suitable AdWords. You can select, delete unwanted or underperforming advertisements, create more advertisements, change wordings of your advertisements, and introduce many improvisations in your advertisements and their presentation.

There is no limit to the number of changes and adjustments in your advertisements. You can keep doing so until you achieve the optimum rate of return from your advertisement. Therefore, an efficient structuring of your AdWords campaign from the beginning can prove helpful. This requires a thorough understanding of your product and effect of AdWords and keywords on your advertisements. Rather, you should know how the keywords link to your product. This can help deliver good results in terms of traffic and resultant increase in sales of your product.

Locate all types of keywords suitable for your product and thereafter categorize them into specific groups like competitive keywords, targeted keywords, not competitive keywords, misspelled keywords, plural keywords and so on.

Create specific and separate advertisements according to the different advertisement groups. This helps in easy identification of the results produced by each group. Make slight variations in the advertisements of each individual group and notice their effect on your traffic.

If you find any particular group not performing well enough, you can delete the particular group. You can alternatively create a new ad group. This helps in trying the effectiveness of your ad group without having to keep changing the keywords to get suitable traffic. Flexibility of the keyword and groups is high.

Google provides all types of pricing options and service levels to suit different categories of budgets and strategies. You can also create hybrid campaigns to suit your marketing approaches and ensure maximum benefits for your product. Your main aim is to increase the traffic at your web site to increase total sales and profits.

Google AdWords has a price structure that bills you only if any client clicks on your advertisement. You do not have to pay Google anything for presenting and displaying your advertisement on the site. Ideally, you pay for the results.

Ten Tips for Managing Your Google AdWords Account

Manage your Google AdWords account with the help of the following tips:

1. Structure your AdWords account according to three levels as Account, Campaign, and Ad Group. This helps in clear demarcation of the different levels and effective coordination.

2. Keep a separate and valid e-mail address for your account with a unique password. This provides confidentiality for all your personal and billing information.

3. The campaign level of your AdWords account contains details of your geographical location, language preferences, daily budgets, distribution preferences, and end dates.

4. The Ad Group level allows you to create suitable advertisements using relevant keywords. You can either have a cost per click for the total Ad Group or for specific and individual keywords.

5. Try to create few ads for each Ad Group and assign separate set of keywords to activate these advertisements. Therefore, every set of Ad Group works with many related keywords. Your advertisements bring in traffic for such targeted keywords.

6. Your AdWords account gives all details of the click through rates at the bottom of each of your advertisements. Analyze performance of every advertisement and delete the nonperforming advertisements. Otherwise, you can also make changes in these advertisements and try them again.

7. Similarly, while grouping your AdWords give adequate importance to the main theme within any particular Ad Group. If the keywords do not display the necessary relevance to the topic, move it to the relevant Ad Group or if unnecessary remove it totally.

8. Proper labeling of your Ad Group ensures easy accessibility and movement between different Ad Groups. You can use the rename button to make any necessary changes in the names of the groups too.

9. Before setting up your AdWords account, go through the relevant tutorial available at the Google web site. This provides adequate information and does away with all doubts while setting up your account.

10. Keyword research proves to be the most important aspect of maintaining your AdWords account. Locating ideal keywords through extensive and focused research can get you targeted keywords.

Keyword Research Basics

Keywords need to be relevant and apt for the products. This is of paramount importance to bring in focused traffic to your web site. Such traffic can transform into paying clients and thereby increase your total sales.

While choosing correct keywords keep a tab that these words are not too broad and vague. Neither should these words be overtly competitive. Then traffic diverts to other related sites and you do not gain from your AdWords campaign. At the same time, a unique keyword may come back with no search results at all.

Therefore, before setting out to select suitable keywords for your product, discuss the variations and details of your products with all concerned.

While focusing on what and how you want to sell your product, you can arrive at many different choices of keywords. Be very specific of your product to receive targeted traffic. Alternatively, you can visit many different online forums. Discussing your product with others gives you a wider and buyer"s perspective of your product.

This is essential to relate to the targeted keywords. You can also visit your competitor"s sites and develop ideas form their presentation of AdWord groups and keywords. However, be careful to avoid their mistakes and concentrate on targeting traffic to your web site. You can check the conversion potential of your keywords. Such research can prove to be a daunting task. However, if you execute it well, you are sure on your path to success.

Keyword Matching Options in Google AdWords

Google offers a pay per click solution to help you advertise your product and benefit from higher traffic at your web site. You have to choose appropriate keyword to benefit from the huge sales. This requires you to choose keywords to suit the targeted audience and their preferences.

Google AdWords offers four different types of matching options. You have to select the appropriate one for your keyword. The different matching options are:

Broad match: This is the default setting for your AdWords campaign. This match means that your advertisement will appear for any combination of the words in your keyword phrase. This match normally brings in lot of traffic with poor conversion rates. You also incur higher costs. However, this match is useful early in the campaign to understand the actual phrases your visitors used to arrive at your site.

Phrase Match: This matching option helps you receive targeted traffic to a certain extent. Your advertisement appears only when the search is according to the particular combination of words in your phrase. If your keyword phrase is "foreign travel," phrase match ensures your advertisement appears only for "foreign travel" and not for "travel foreign." Place keyword within quotation marks to denote this match. Phrase matching is in between broad match and exact match as it offers better flexibility than broad match but less than exact match.

Exact Match: Exact match poses no ambiguity. You advertisement appears only if there is an exact match of the keyword. Place keyword phrase within [] brackets to denote exact match option. This delivers the best traffic and the type you want to receive too.

Negative Match: If you do not want your keyword to appear in any particular keyword phrase match results, use this match. List your keyword phrase with a (-) in front to denote negative match. This helps in keeping junk traffic away from your AdWords campaign.

The best combination of keyword matching could be to include broad and phrase match to exact match. Negative matching can help keep unrelated traffic at bay.

How to Find Inexpensive Keywords

Keywords form the base of your advertising on Google AdWords. These decide your rankings and the cost of advertising on Google AdWords. There are two main types of keywords, expensive and non-expensive. You need to understand the correlation between these two to get the best of your advertisements.

A thorough knowledge of keyword pricing is essential to understand the effect of advertising through pay per click search engines and other affiliate marketing businesses too. You can earn good profits if you are able to decide and choose the correct keyword with the appropriate pricing too.

There are many inexpensive keywords available. Some of these inexpensive keywords could be variations of your main or primary keyword. Use these inexpensive keywords in many places of your advertisement to benefit from low advertising costs through pay per click.

Inexpensive keywords are just a combination of the original keywords in many different ways. Initially, you may not be able to judge the suitability of any particular keyword. Try different combinations among many hundreds of keywords. Thereafter, you can single out the nonperforming keywords.

Elimination of unnecessary and rather nonperforming keywords can lower your bid price and increase your sales. Increased sales also affect your click through rate and your advertising expenses. The key to locate and benefit from inexpensive keywords is to test the effectiveness of any keyword. Testing can be through your own market testing techniques or through Google"s tools.

Another major factor in play is the effect of such inexpensive keywords on the traffic at your web site. Previously your site could have had advertisements of any particular keyword. If now you increase traffic by using many inexpensive keywords, the present traffic may not be as focused and targeted as the earlier one. Such change in the character of traffic at your web site can cast its effect on your advertisements.

Change in the character of traffic at your web site can increase or decrease your rankings. Therefore, before choosing any inexpensive keywords, you have to watch its effect on your advertisements and resultant sales and profits too.

Increasing Your Clickthrough and Conversion Rates with Negative Keywords

Negative match keyword is the best way to prevent your advertisement from appearing if search includes any keyword irrelevant to your advertisement. A (-) sign before the keyword denotes negative match.

Negative match keywords help you avoid unwanted traffic at your web site. This increases your click through rate and delivers targeted traffic. Therefore, you do not pay for unwanted clicks. Hence, your advertisement costs are lower. Conversion rates are high and targeted.

Negative match helps you control the traffic viewing your advertisement. Therefore, only genuinely interested and focused traffic access your web site and advertisement. Proper manipulation of the matching options at Google AdWords delivers excellent results for your web traffic.

Seasonal Keywords

It is common to witness wide fluctuations in clicks at different times of the year according to the seasons. Some of your keywords could be very popular at particular time of the year. These are seasonal keywords. This is possible even if you do not make any special arrangements and changes in your web site to accommodate the seasonal fluctuations.

If your web site puts up greeting cards, you can witness an increase in clicks and high advent of traffic during the approach of any holiday season like Christmas, New Year, Easter, Halloween, and Valentine"s Day. You can put up promotional offers for sports seasons, tourist seasons, and others. You can open a small window during the gift seasons through targeted keywords. This window can help focus on a short-term campaign. Such seasonal keywords receive much number of hits and your click through rate is considerably low.

You can operate these special web pages with seasonal keywords for around three to four weeks. Thereafter, you can take them off. However, this lowers possibilities of indexing by search engines. Therefore, it is better to keep these pages permanently on your web site.

You can provide separate links to every additional page from the bottom of your site-map. Such a regular presentation can allow search engines to assess them regularly and rank you at higher levels accordingly.

Keywords that May Attract Click Defrauders

Keyword spamming is a popular technique of defrauders. Such spamming refers to forceful intervention into your keyword titles or other descriptions. Spammers place brand names into your title to grab all attention.

Excessive use of keywords can also lead to spam. Keyword density beyond 6% is more prone to being spam. Sensible use of keywords can help stay within the requisite keyword density and get a good ranking on the search engine too.

To safeguard yourself against click defrauders, maintain a close watch on the click rates on your web site regularly. If you witness any sudden drop or if the clicks fall beyond statistical averages, you should investigate into the problem.

International fraud mainly exists if you have any content–specific advertisements in third-party sites. There could be links from these sites to many different companies recruiting staff to click at these web sites. Another way of evading such click defrauders is to increase your keyword base to contain many relevant and specific terms. This can reduce click fraud largely.

Using negative keywords is another powerful technique to avoid click defrauders. Google AdSense can then display products and services unrelated to yours. You can further track the relevant URL to locate the traffic arriving at your web site.

Regular reviewing of server logs with the help of other applications like Click tracks and Click Defense can help you monitor click fraud levels.

Use of Illegal Keywords

You have to plan and think before registering your domain name. Some domain names could include trademarked keywords. It is then illegal for you to use such a domain name as it can easily create confusion in the mind of the customer. Similarly, using such trademarked keywords in your Meta tags is also illegal. Again, if you use such keywords for any illegal purpose, others could sue you. Google has to refrain from advertising sponsored links, if involved in legal suits or any such illegal trademark queries.

Google encourages advertisers and trademark owners to settle their disputes within themselves. The same advertiser could have similar advertisements on many other search engines. However, Google does perform limited amount of investigation too.

Google AdWords does not allow sale of trademarks as keywords. Recently, though Google has brought in a major change in policy specifically for Canada and U.S. It now allows advertisers to include trademarked titles and similar terms in their keywords and advertisements on their web pages.

Nevertheless, you cannot use others" trademarks in your advertisements. Your ad can appear when someone searches for Nike.

However, you cannot advertise discount sales of Nike shoes. Google wants to discontinue use of continuous keywords too. Trademark owners could impose restrictions on use of certain trademarks as the ad text of your advertisement. Sometimes such restrictions are in force within specific geographical boundaries.

Which Keywords are More Profitable?

It is necessary to maintain necessary density of your keyword in your articles. Using the correct keyword offers greater chances of a higher ranking by the search engines. Obviously, higher ranking ensures higher traffic and increase in sales and profits. Therefore, keywords hold the main reins. You can develop better and more profitable keywords to score over your competitors. If you share your keywords with other competitors, you cannot benefit from increase in traffic. Therefore, you have to adopt viable techniques to come up with profitable keywords.

How to Locate Keywords That is More Profitable?

The best way to arrive at such profitable keywords is to become a visitor at your own web site. This helps you view your web site through the eyes of an outsider. You have to type in words in the search engine box just like your visitors. Again, try to use slightly offbeat phrases to locate good keywords. Few examples include "buy sports books online" in place of "eBooks" or "moneymaker machine" in place of "lucrative affiliate program".

Thereafter make use of the Search Term Suggestion Tool at your web site to get an idea of the number of times the particular term was in use or searched recently. This projects an idea of the demand position of the word. It is better to avoid single word keywords and stress on keyword phrases. These phrases deliver more focused and targeted traffic.

The best and most profitable keywords are those with a high demand but low supply. These words can boost your web traffic to great heights. If there are many competitors for your product, you have to place more stress on less obvious keywords. These keywords have very low supply and demand too. Search engines rank you high on such keywords.

It is an illusion that expensive keyword could be a very profitable keyword. This is because of the low volume of traffic. Ideally, the best way to locate keywords that are more profitable is by ranking the cost of the keyword by the cost of clicks per day in place of rating the cost of each click.

How to Write Profitable Google

AdWords Ads

Writing a proper Google AdWords ad can help transform it into a profitable ad. Profitable ads assure you of good returns and higher profits through better sales. Few guidelines can help you devise a profitable Google AdWords ad.

Choosing Correct Keywords - Place your keywords within appropriate brackets to help search engines target the correct keyword phrase. Your ad will not show for any other combination of keywords other than specifically mentioned.

Choosing the correct audience - Your ad has to reach the correct audience to generate the best response. You have to choose the relevant countries and their respective languages to garner necessary support and popularity.

Highlighted Keywords - Include your keyword in the title and advertisement description. Google highlights the searched keywords. This helps users to locate searched keywords soon. Include such searched keywords to attract more traffic.

Test your Ads - Conduct a simultaneous check over two or more of your ads. This helps you know the higher click ratio of the tested ads to make necessary amends.

Conversion Ratio - Conversion ratio is essential to judge the viability of your ad. This ratio projects the number of conversions of your leads into actual sales. You can then calculate how far beneficial the ad is to you. Although Google does not offer any such tracking for conversion ratio, you can use a special tacking link with an affiliate tracking system.

Consolidate Attention - Your ad should be able to consolidate attention from all quarters. Try to use words attracting attention like free, new, and similar others.

Sell your Ad - You have to spell out the benefits of your product in your ad like lose weight, earn money, and similar others.

Use Power words - Power words can evoke strong emotions in the minds of the customers. Some of them include free trial, Special offer, Limited offer, free shipping, and others. You can formulate these words into specific action phrases evoking immediate action.

Do away with common words - Do not use simple words like a, an, the, and others in your keyword phrase.

Landing Page - It is important to have a correct and assured link to your landing page. This evokes greater interest in the customer than landing at the home page of your web site from the link.

How to Write Ads that Attract Clicks

Your pay per click campaign is culmination of many different steps eventually leading to your advertisement. Each of these steps has a certain objective for conveying the correct meaning and purpose in the advertisement. Therefore, writing effective advertisements to draw targeted clicks at your web site is only a part of the whole process.

Keyword listing increases your click through rate by fifty percent. Follow certain basic guidelines to write advertisements that can bring in relevant traffic.

Focus: Every advertisement has many subtopics. Therefore, your keyword lists should include all details of these subtopics. A broad purview of your product does not deliver focused attention. If you deal in personal loans and your advertisement has the keyword loans, obviously most of the traffic to your site may not be that useful. Therefore, a basic idea of the product with specific emphasis on your type of product can be a better advertisement.

Conversion Rate: Your advertisement should end in profitable conversions. Otherwise, you only incur the cost of the advertisement without getting any benefit from it. Your advertisement should be persuasive and deliver factual results of the search.

Connecting Links: Each of your advertisement should contain relevant and correct links to suitable sites. Therefore, a proper landing page can help your advertisement arrive at the correct site. This also translates into potential clients. Otherwise, it is a waste of clicks.

Clear Perspective: Before writing your advertisement, you should have a clear conception of your product. Also, have a clear understanding of the requisites of the market and your client.

Negative Keywords: These keywords can help increase the focus of your advertisement. Negative keywords single out unnecessary information about your product and make your advertisements more effective. This does away with unwanted clicks too.

Therefore, the ideal advertisement should have the following parts –

- A catchy headline

- First line conveying the most powerful benefit

- Second line providing justification of your action though the most powerful feature of your product

How to Optimize Your Google AdWords Ads

Your advertisements through pay per click should deliver optimized results leading to an increase in the click through rates. This delivers maximum returns on your investment and lowers advertisement costs. This also increases your conversion ratios thereby increasing your overall profits.

Effective tips to increase optimization of your Google AdWords advertisements are –

Relevant Advertisements - Write out many different types of advertisements for the same product. Test your advertisement on the site. Thereafter change the headline and test its effectiveness and conversion ratios. Note the change in conversions to assess the viability and effectiveness of any particular format of your advertisement.

Traffic - Traffic at your site should be focused and relevant. Therefore, include targeted words to point at particular features of your product. This ensures appropriate and significant traffic at your web site. This eventually optimizes your advertisement and increases conversion rates.

Landing Page - A landing page offers your clients direct access to the related web page. Your page headline, correct and relevant links, and focused reviews improve effectiveness of your advertisement. Include pictures of your product with interesting reviews adding content to your advertisement. Illustrations also prove helpful.

Discounts and Freebies - Free offers and similar other contests or prizes attract many. Such incentives in your advertisement draw the attention of the client to visit your link and arrive at the relevant site. Although this could draw many clients and customers, many come for the freebies. However, you can benefit through such increase in conversions.

Client Information - Include the form containing client information, e-mail address and other preferences. Maintain full confidentiality of all these details and build up customer relationships. Convincing the customer is essential to increase conversion rates.

Simplicity - Explain details and utility of your product in simple and explicit terms without use of excessive language. Do not keep away facts. Simple and clear dealing leads to increased click through rates increasing your sales, consequently lowering your costs.

Tracking - Google AdWords provides a simple tracking facility to analyze movement of your advertisement. Maintain a close watch over performing and nonperforming keywords. Deleting nonperforming ones can increase effectiveness and optimization of your advertisements.

Destination Page Optimization

Optimization of your page is essential to rank high on the search engines. Although keywords, titles, and other write-ups do contribute to the ranking on the search engines, yet optimization of the page holds the key for maximum benefits.

Content of your page is the determining factor for ranking on the search engines. Good content with liberal use of keywords are a hit with webmasters. Search engines evaluate your page from the initial few lines of the text on page.

Publish your web site as a static HTML site as this offers better opportunities to work and present. These pages download faster and search engines find indexing your website easier with few HTML codes. Ideally, a 50 KB page with graphics poses the correct weight. More than 100 KB makes it slower and some search engines avoid such heavy pages.

A short title tag with around eight to ten words is the best. The title should contain and point to the most important content in the page. The name of your organization and your product does not hold any place in the title. Few phrases with keywords and descriptions of the pictures also rank high with search engines. Search engine professionals can help formulate and implement guidelines to optimize your pages to the maximum. This ensures excellent performance and ranking of your site at all times.

Google AdWords Pricing System

Google is the most popular search engine on the Internet and advertising on Google will get you guaranteed business. Google AdWords is a good way to get the desired publicity for your business. Using this facility, you can place your advertisements on pages based on the keyword searches.

The AdWords pricing depends on location of the advertisement on the page. The text AdWords are more effective than banner advertisements. Google AdWords will place your advertisements depending on the clicks for ten to fifteen dollars per thousand advertisements. Let us now understand pricing of Google AdWords. Google charges you on a click per keyword basis. You must bid for every click depending on your daily budget. This is the maximum cost per click. Google will adjust this cost depending on the number of daily clicks and the quality score.

Quality score is the composite score of your keyword"s importance and its past performance. This determines the minimum bid amount for your keyword that will generate advertisements. You may need to increase the cost per click if it is less than the minimum bid. So, select high quality keywords for your advertisements to minimize your promotional costs.

Google adopts a different pricing for its content pages. If you place your advertisement on a page with a less chance of a sale, then Google will charge you less for advertising on that page. Google also helps you make a daily budget for your keywords that ensures maximum visibility. You can change this amount whenever you want.

In case your keyword gets more clicks than you paid for, then Google adjusts it by giving you an over delivery credit. Thus the Google Ad words pricing system is flexible enough to give the advertisers sufficient coverage within their budget.

How to Set the Maximum Cost Per Click

Cost per click is the money you pay to Google when a user clicks on your advertisement. Therefore, you must bid for keywords depending on your target audience and the cost you are willing to pay per click for the selected keyword. The advantage of this method is that you refine your advertisement and reach your target audience effectively. You have full control over the promotional budget and the keywords. This promotional method is affordable and very effective if used properly.

When you use Google Ad words, you have to specify the amount that you are willing to pay per click. For this use keywords that are popular but affordable. The most popular keywords will get you only a few clicks a day, within your limited daily budget. Therefore, you can choose the second rung of keywords that are cheaper, but as effective in getting traffic to your website. To decide the maximum cost per click visit the Google website and use the traffic estimator for your list of keywords. This estimator will give you the maximum clicks possible for your keyword in a day. These traffic estimates may vary daily, and you may get lesser clicks than projected. You can change the number of clicks and then select the most suitable keywords within your budget. Concentrate on getting a few higher end clicks, than many lower end clicks, as they do not lead to sales.

You may have to try out different keywords and the response to them to get an idea of the optimum keywords. Do not use the name of your firm as the keyword. Instead, make the keyword the solution to your customer"s problems for better impact. You must assess the clicks per keywords to check the conversion rate. You should also check periodically if your keywords rank high on Google searches. You can set the maximum cost per click by dividing the expected profit per sale by the number of expected clicks per sale. This method is good if you want fast sales. However, you must not exceed your budget and design the cost per click promotions thoughtfully for maximum impact.

How to Set Your Daily and Monthly Budget

While advertising for your product or service through Google AdWords ad, you need to set specific daily and monthly budgets. Your advertising budget depends on your limitations. You have therefore to decide how much you can spend on advertisements. It could be a lump sum amount for a month or depend on how many times your advertisement is clicked without having any specific ceiling on the budget.

Google AdWords provides you a specific tool to evaluate the amount of your total budget given a specific target amount each day. Google normally charges five cents for active words or phrases. Every campaign has a minimum monthly budget of $15. You can set the maximum targets and click rates for every URL. Accordingly decide on the minimum amount of deposit necessary for maintaining your advertisement on Google AdWords campaign.

A little experimentation with the keywords can provide an outline of the advertisement expenditures. Google also suggests recommended budgets. Nevertheless, you can decide on the amount you want to spend on advertisements. You can set a specific amount as your daily budget.

Google displays your ad as long as the daily budget is available. As soon as it exhausts, Google stops display of your ad. The next day, it again starts display according to your budget for the day. However, Google spreads the ads over the day and does not exhaust everything during any particular part of the day.

Start with a higher budget for your well-written ads. Your costs per click are higher and you receive good ranking position too. Try to achieve a click through rate of four to seven percent. Thereafter, gradually lower your costs per click (CPC) while retaining your high daily budget on advertisement costs. A lower CPC does not then affect your click through rate anymore.

A low daily budget will display your advertisements only intermittently. To enhance better search results for your keywords, use exact matches, negative keywords, adjusting bids, and target region wise. Although the lower limit of a daily budget for an ad is $0.01, there is no upper limit.

Ten Tips on Successful Pricing Strategies

Pricing refers to fixing of the optimum cost of your goods or services. Your price should cover all your costs of production, marketing, advertising, distribution, and provide for adequate profit too. However, price should be affordable and well within the competition.

Ten tips for successful pricing strategies include -

1. Price of your product should be in line with that of your competitors. Customers normally feel low priced goods are low in quality. Therefore, conduct necessary research before fixing the price of your goods and services to arrive at the best optimum price.

2. Always provide the best service to your customer when you receive any call or e-mail for a quote or an estimate. Instant and spontaneous service yields great benefits in

the form of sales. Your customer would not mind paying slightly high rates for excellent and prompt service.

3. Calculate your profit margins regularly and give due consideration to all changes in expense and other overheads. Nevertheless, you should always maintain a specific profit margin.

4. While calculating your costs or profits, do not give much importance to hourly rates or costs. These may sound reasonable. However, if you calculate the rates for the total number of hours you put into your business. It could turn out to be very low and may not offer a good profit margin. Therefore, give due credence to all the different costs.

5. When your customers ask for your prices, state them equivocally. Do not try to defend or justify your prices. You also do not have to present the breakup of your prices.

6. Fix your fees at a slightly higher rate at the initial stages. You can lower your charges later.

7. There are many different options available to maintain your profit margins and provide flexibility in your pricing. You can adopt different packages of pricing by time, projects, hour schedule, and others.

8. You can offer free initial consultations or necessary sales presentations. However, keep such consultations and presentations within a specified limit. Alternatively, another beneficial pricing strategy is to fix a charge for your initial consultation or presentation. However, your customer pays for this only if he buys your product. You can then include such fees in the final invoice. Sometimes negotiating your price and yielding a little to the pressures of your customer could be the best move.

9. Another pricing strategy hints at including small charges for services provided after completion of the sale.

10. Ideally analyzing your worth in the market in comparison to your competitors proves useful in arriving at the best pricing module.

Such practical pricing strategies can help resolve many pricing issues and you can overcome your past mistakes too.

Tracking Ads and Landing Pages

Tracking of your advertisements is essential to understand performance of your advertisements. Tracking ads essentially means to evaluate reaction of the visitors after they arrive at your page. These trackers judge the reactions and interest levels of visitors as they go through your web site.

Therefore, landing pages prove to be the major connector between your advertisement and your visitor. Landing page refers to the page you arrive at by clicking at the link provided in the ad. This page provides total information of your product or service. Experts differ in their view over what essentially should be on the landing page. It should place sufficient importance on the actual content of the page and include a brief idea of any other offers available at your site. You can do well by experimenting and analyzing what factors lead to an increase in traffic at your web site. You benefit the most with targeted and focused traffic. Trackers can locate the particular point beyond which your customers do not proceed in your web site. These also locate the effective keywords and prevent any theft or fraud at your web site.

While planning your landing page, try to include all possible information. Thereafter condense the total content placing maximum importance on the core elements. This can help in increasing traffic leading to high conversion rates.

Destination Pages that Increase Your Profits

Destination page refers to the landing page of any link in your advertisement. Your destination pages should remain the same overall but consist of regular updates about necessary information. Changing your destination pages regularly cannot increase profits. Ideally, your destination page should be a working web site. If advertisement lands on an empty or an invalid site, you lose on your lead and eventually a customer. Similarly, linking to landing pages or sites under construction will also dissuade your potential customers.

The best way to increase your profits is to offer good and reliable links and landing pages for your advertisements. Your customers will perceive the value of the content in your destination page.

Again, there should not be any elaborate programs and further clicks to arrive at the definite landing page. It should also be in an HTML format. Proper guidelines can link your customers clicking on your AdWords to their destinations.

To benefit from higher profits, your links need to have destination pages with high conversion rates. This can boost your profits substantially. Ideally, your landing or destination page should have a provision for finalizing the sale process. Therefore, a buy now or purchase button in the landing page can bring about a sale. Otherwise, just signing up for a free newsletter can also help in cementing the relationship with your customer and you could build up on this relationship later.

How to Improve Your Keyword Click-Through-Rate (CTR)

Click through rate is the number of people ho actually click on your advertisement. Keywords play an important role in your Internet advertising strategy. Therefore, you must choose keywords such that they give you the maximum possible click through. This will help you reach the desired target audience and lower your cost per click.

You must pay great attention to improve your click through rate to get the best return on your investment. A rate of .05%is respectable enough for Google to run your advertisement. You must select good keywords that are not generic for greater impact. Use related keywords that address your target audience for greater impact. Try to include the product or service that you are offering in the keyword phrase. To stand out from competition will get you a better click use a specific keyword phrase that through rate. Use high quality keywords for maximum response to your advertisement. Use the Google tools together all linked keywords under an Ad group and then make specifically targeted advertisements using these keywords. This strategy will definitely improve your click through rate.

To get the best response to your advertisement, use specific keywords that will match the searches entered by users of the search engine. This will give you more credit and drive down your cost per click. If you use a variable title, it improves your click through rate by more than hundred percent. If the user finds his keywords in your advertisement then your click through rate improves.

Google lets you use variable destination URL. This lets you know what the user is searching, so you can modify the content of your website to match the searched items. This leads to a better conversion rate and helps improve traffic to your website.

A good click through rate is very important so you get a good response to your advertisement in the form of purchases or sales leads. A good click through rate will improve your presence on the Internet and get the desired response form your target audience. If you have a high click through rate your position and rankings on the search pages improves. Google specifies that your advertisements must be relevant so that you get more clicks. A higher ranking implies you can reduce your promotional expense. Customers are always on the lookout for freebies. Therefore, if you add an incentive to your advertisement, customers will definitely click on your advertisement. Present your product or service as a solution to the customer"s problem. This will tempt him to click on your advertisement. These simple tips can help you improve the click through rate on a small budget and get a good return on your investment.

What is a Testing Process?

A testing process gives you an idea of performance of your advertisement. Every site offers different opportunities and therefore, regular testing can help you understand the effectiveness of your advertisement. This can help you adopt different techniques and other remedial measures to bring in more focused and targeted traffic. The testing is ideally between two different pages and is therefore popular as split testing. You have to carry out the test for a long period to generate a sample size of your advertisement. Normally, fifty actions for a single page or at least a thousand visitors can form a sample.

Besides, it is a comparison between two pages. Hence, if one of the pages receives less number of visitors while the other completes 1,000 visitors, you can analyze the cause for such differences. Both the pages need to present competitive ideas and your customers have to judge the better of the two.

You can just change the headline and keep the same text to create two different pages. Once you are able to understand which of your pages or advertisement has a better rating, try to increase the time of that particular ad. Always try to use the target keyword in your headline and include the biggest benefit within the headline too. Use strong words inducing action like right now, save now, and others. Use Capital letters for the first letter of each word in the headline.

Why Testing Your Google AdWords Ads is So Important

You have many different advertisement copies for your web page. These different pages are just variations of the same text and differ mainly in presentation of facts. Therefore, split testing between these pages can help you understand the target market and project the most effective page.

Such testing is very important as it brings into focus the exact picture of your ad. The testing process is very scientific and it eliminates results until you arrive at the perfect results. Such testing helps you reduce your advertisement costs drastically.

You can avoid the competitive bids of your competitors and maintain a proper position through the number of click through. You can garner a better rate of return through additional marketing and pay per click rates. You can lower your bid amount and still maintain the number of click through. Further, such testing improves your brand name and you benefit through additional clicks on your URL. Google normally shows only the better ad on its pages. Google normally notifies if your advertisement is performing below standard. It removes the ad and does not display it. You need to make necessary changes for projecting it again. Testing can help save this situation. Every site is different from other sites and has a unique position and acclaim of its own. Therefore, regular testing and experimentation of your ads is essential to have a clear picture of your standing.

How to Use Google's Conversion Tracking and Other Tracking Software

Conversion tracking is to follow the action of a client at your web site. Ideally, this hints at the customer joining an e-mail newsletter, placing an order, downloading software and others. Tracking of such conversions is essential to gauge performance of your product and your online business too. This gives you an idea of the origin of your customers, which is useful in many other endeavors.

Pay per click campaign does not offer any help in tracking your sales. Conversion software at Google helps you track your client and get an idea of the effective and ineffective keywords. You can let go of such ineffective keywords and use only the effective ones. Different web sites use different tools to monitor performance of your web site.

Conversion tracking software helps in optimization of the landing page. You can choose effective conversion techniques to maximize your popularity on Google AdWords.

Conversion tracking software also helps with different e-mail marketing tools. This provides information about the specific URLs in your tracking campaigns and identifies links leading to effective sales. You can also compare different marketing tools and mailing through their revenue generation, conversion rates, and other relevant parameters.

Conversion tracking helps you gather information about certain sites connecting to your site. These sites could be sending excellent traffic to your site. This helps in developing better business opportunities with such sites.

Ten Tips for Correct Test Results with Google AdWords

Testing of ad copies on the pay per click search engines is essential to arrive at an optimum click through rate. Google AdWords makes it possible to have many different ads for the same group. You have to test the effectiveness of these ads.

Ten tips for arriving at the correct test results with Google AdWords include -

1. Test key phrases and short sentences by breaking up your advertisement texts. Such testing takes less time and produces fast results. It also delivers accurate results.

2. Micro testing techniques can deliver correct results of your advertisement tests. You can take help from previous case studies and other research too. Nevertheless, micro

testing between two different products delivers fast results.

3. The headline of your advertisement text holds the key for success of your advertisement. Ideally, testing the headline can deliver accurate results of your success rate with Google AdWords. A catchy headline containing key information about your product can increase your click through rate extensively.

4. After analyzing the appropriate keyword phrase for your Google AdWords, test the effectiveness of different texts with the same keyword phrase. Small changes in your advertisement can bring about a new headline and text.

5. It is best to test many different ads simultaneously. This is split testing. Such testing can help you arrive at the highest click through ratio possible.

6. To benefit from good ads, improvise on the ads performing poorly. Sometimes a single word or just a change in arrangement of words can deliver your message more effectively and success rate of your advertisement shoots up. Google then rates your advertisement very high.

7. While conducting split testing, be aware that not all tests may yield correct and positive results. Sometime, you may have to repeat the test while at other times you may have to adopt different measures totally.

8. Split testing requires you to conduct many tests to arrive at the correct results. These tests may take well over a fortnight to deliver results. Cost is also another major factor in split testing.

9. Multivariate testing is also an effective mode of arriving at the correct results of your Google AdWords. Such testing

7912191R00059

Printed in Great Britain
by Amazon.co.uk, Ltd.,
Marston Gate.